Contents

Introduction	2
Herb garden	3
Terminology	4
Decoction	4
Infusion	4
Tincture	4
Ointment	4
Poultice	4
Cream	4
Healing herbs	5
Garlic	5
Fungal infections	5
Stomach	5
Research	6
Cholesterol	6
Cancer	6
Diabetes	6
Suggestions	6
Notes	6
Turmeric	7
Digestion	7
Travel	7
Circulation	7
Skin conditions	7
Research	8
Liver	8
Caution	8
Peppermint	9
Indigestion	9
Flatulence	9
Tension headache	9
Nausea	9
Fevers	10
Nasal congestion	10
Caution	10
Lavender	10
Depression	10
Sleeplessness	10
Antiseptic	11
Asthma	11
Digestion	11
Caution	11
Celery	11
Detoxifying	12
Disinfection	12
Circulation	12
Chest infections	12
Blood pressure	12
Caution	12
Thyme	13
Candles	13
Essential oil	13

Hay fever and asthma	13
Back pain	1
Caution	1
Ginseng	1
Adaption	14
Stress	14
Memory	14
Sleep problems	14
Sugar levels	15
Stamina	15
Cautions	15
St John's wort	15
Nervous problems	15
Hormones	15
Bites	15
Cramps	16
Ulcers	16
Infections	16
Caution	16
Holy basil	16
Invigoration	16
Stress	16
Diabetes	17
Coughs and sneezes	17
Ayurvedic medicine	17
White willow	17
Headaches	17
Hot conditions	18
Mobility	18
Caution	18
Elder	18
Colds	18
Constipation	18
Hay fever	19
Catarrh	19
Caution	19
Ginger	19
Trapped wind	19
Cancer	19
Travel sickness	20
Colds and flu	20
Research	20
Heart	20
Caution	21
Echinacea	21
Colds and flu	21
Stimulation	21
Respiratory illnesses	21
AIDS and HIV	21
Infections	22
Research	22
Caution	22
Sage	22
Mouth	22

Expectorant	24
Adrenal glands	24
Arthritis	24
Caution	24
Aloe vera	24
Cleopatra	25
Irritable bowel syndrome	25
Laxative	25
Burns, grazes and scalds	25
Diabetes	25
All-rounder	25
Cautions	25
Figwort	26
Anti-inflammatory	26
Burns and swelling	26
Pain	26
Caution	26
Rosemary	26
Stimulation	26
Rheumatism	26
Digestion	27
Nervous tension	27
Hair tonic	27
Caution	27
Herbs for children	27
Anxiety and stress	27
Chickenpox and measles	27
Colds	28
Lice	28
Diarrhoea	28
Colic	28
Teething	28
Cooking	29
Care and caution	29
Final words	30

Introduction

This book has been a delight to write. It is an informal guide in which I have collated the healing properties of various herbs and coupled them with scientific research from hospitals, news and research institutes.

Also included are suggestions and tips from healers and users of herbal medicine from around the globe. These have been collected via my website over the last two years.

Whether you are looking for herbal remedies for yourself or someone else, the way to use this book is the same:

1. Determine whether there is a herb that is relevant to the condition you are interested in.

2. Seek the advice of your physician as to whether the herb will be beneficial for you and whether it will affect any other medication you are taking.

3. Find a recognised and reputable herbalist and get their opinion on the herb and your condition (a good herbalist will always work in conjunction with your physician).

Throughout this book you will find suggestions made to me via my website. Where possible I have tried to supplement these tips and tales by verifying the information. You will find this information in the endnotes.

Remember! You are paying good money for your doctor and herbalists – so ask questions. And once you have asked them – ask them again!

An important aspect of this book is that it gives control of your health back to the only person who really has it in the first place; you!

Herb lore is ancient in its origins and yet in its infancy as it is being rediscovered by medical researchers.

This booklet brings both of these sources (herb lore and scientific research) together so that you can judge for yourself whether a herb is suitable for you.

Finding out about herbs, growing them, preparing them and using them is an activity that is blessed in many ways, consider for a moment that by these activities you are:

- Taking control of your health and well-being
- Gaining new and fascinating insights into the world you are living in
- Building self-confidence
- Enhancing your connections with the devic (natural) world

Scientists are examining the sites of ancient hospitals in order to learn about the herbs that were used at the time.

The benefits of herbs are numerous as I hope you will discover as you read this book. To be going on with, however, just let me mention a few of them. Herbs can:

- Help with skin conditions
- Lower sugar levels
- Aid respiratory problems
- Soothe inflammations
- Fight infections
- Help wounds heal faster
- Aid circulation
- Help the immune system

As I mentioned, these are just a few of the ailment that herbs are useful for. Please use the contents page to help you search for a suitable remedy.

I hope that you enjoy this book as much as I did in writing it. Please take a few minutes to visit my website and contribute your healing stories.

www.healingbooks.net

Herb garden

There is nothing like the satisfaction of growing and using your own herbs. The activity of growing and nurturing your own plants or herbs gives 'herbal healing' a whole new dimension.

It is the simplest thing to grow your own herbs, even for those who do not have a garden. Using a window box or even small flowerpots is sufficient for your needs.

My advice in any endeavour is to start small. Thyme, sage and basil are herbs that are easy to grow, so why not start with these?

Terminology

Now that you are stepping into the world of herbology it is good to know what some of the terms mean:

Decoction

Some parts of herbs, for example roots and bark, require forceful treatment to extract their medicinal essences. A decoction involves simmering such parts for 20 to 30 minutes and then sieving the contents into a jug.

Infusion

This is just like making tea. Place 1 tsp of dried herb or 2 tsp of fresh herb (or combination of herbs) into a cup. Fill with boiled water, cover and infuse for 5 to 10 minutes.

Tincture

These are made by soaking the herb in alcohol to give a relatively stronger action than infusions or decoctions. Tinctures can last up to 2 years. 35% vodka is an ideal alcohol strength to use.

Ointment

These contain oil or fats heated with herbs. They do not contain water and so form a separate layer on the skin. They protect against injury or inflammation and carry active medical constituents to the affected area. Ointments can be made from several bases but the most common is petroleum jelly.

Poultice

A poultice is a mixture of fresh, dried or powdered herbs that is applied to an affected area. They are often used to ease nerve or muscle pains, sprains, or broken bones; they are also used to draw out pus from infected wounds.

Cream

These are similar to poultices but have water added to them. Creams have the benefit of blending with the skin, allowing it to breathe, are cooling and soothing.

Healing herbs

In the following pages I am going to go over the healing properties of several common herbs. I hope that you are surprised by the medicinal effects of herbs that are easily available and indeed that are often used in culinary dishes.

Garlic

- Latin name: *Allium sativum*
- Lowers blood pressure
- Antibiotic
- Expectorant[1]
- Anti-diabetic
- Reduces cholesterol

Garlic is often used in treatments of internal and external viral, bacterial and fungal infections.

> Huge quantities of garlic were used in the First World War to disinfect wounds and prevent gangrene; just as the Roman army used it 2000 years ago.

Fungal infections

When applied externally can help fight fungal infections such as vaginal thrush and athlete's foot. Also helps to clean infected wounds.

> Garlic thins the blood and so is good for those who have heart related problems – if you are taking medication for blood thinning e.g. aspirin, then check with your doctor to see if taking a more natural remedy, i.e. garlic, is better for you. *Phyllis, USA*

Stomach

Regular garlic intake is also beneficial for sluggish (wind and bloating) digestion, especially in older people.

> Garlic is great for intestinal parasite infections.[2] It also aids in getting rid of gastroenteritis and dysentery problems. *Karen, UK*

5

Research

Researchers have for many years been trying to get to the bottom of garlic and its healing abilities. This is not surprising since it is one of the biggest selling herbs in the world.[3]

Here are a couple of properties that you should know about.

Cholesterol

The largest study[4] of garlic was conducted in Germany where 261 patients from 30 general practices were given either garlic powder tablets or a placebo. After a 12-week treatment period average serum cholesterol levels dropped by 12% in the garlic treated group and triglycerides dropped by 17% compared with the placebo group.

Cancer

Several case-control studies,[5] in which the diets of cancer patients are compared with the diets of healthy individuals, have linked Allium vegetables to reduced risks for cancer of the stomach, colon, oesophagus, breast and lining of the uterus (but check though, because some reports say that garlic negates the effects of cancer drugs).

Diabetes

Garlic is known to stabilise blood sugar levels and hence is good for Type 2 diabetics.[6]

After consultation with my doctor I decided to take garlic supplements instead of medication. This, coupled with a regime of exercise and 'correct' food intake, has kept my sugar levels under control for the last two years.
Leila, USA

Suggestions

Chopped garlic in food preparations reduces cholesterol and boosts the immune system.

Gilroy, California claims to be the Garlic Capital of the World[7]

Notes

- Garlic can irritate people with a sensitive digestion.
- To help reduce 'garlic breath' eat an apple after taking garlic or chew a sprig of parsley or a few cardamom seeds.

- Garlic can interfere with the operation of some medical drugs, in particular anti-coagulants – please consult your doctor before taking garlic remedies.

Turmeric

- Latin name: *Curcuma longa*
- Anti-inflammatory
- Eases stomach pain
- Eases nausea and travel sickness
- Stimulates secretion of bile
- Anti-bacterial

Digestion

Turmeric is an excellent herb for relieving gastritis and acidity. The herb helps by increasing mucus production and protects the stomach.

To treat such conditions, mix turmeric into an infusion, tea for example. add some honey to sweeten. A daily dosage would be about ¼ or ½ teaspoon, two or three times a day.

Travel

Turmeric is also said to alleviate travel sickness and nausea, as is its cousin, ginger. Take a couple of ginger sweets with you when next travelling or a packet of ginger biscuits.

Ayurvedic and Chinese medicines both suggest turmeric for improving the action of the liver and for treating jaundice.

Circulation

Since turmeric is an anti-inflammatory and has cholesterol lowering as well as blood thinning properties it is an excellent herb for those who are at risk from strokes and heart disease.

Skin conditions

Psoriasis and athlete's foot can be treated with turmeric paste.

Take one teaspoon of turmeric and mix it with some water and then apply the paste to the skin. *Angie, Germany*.

Research

It is beginning to appear that turmeric may be helpful for neurological disorders like Alzheimer's disease – one finding suggested that Asians (who eat more curries and hence more turmeric) had less incidences of Alzheimer's than non-Asians.

A team from the University of California at Los Angeles[8] believes that turmeric may play a role in slowing down the progression of the neurodegenerative disease.

Alzheimer's is linked to the build-up of knots in the brain called amyloid plaques. Turmeric reduced the number of these plaques by a half.

The US Cystic Fibrosis Foundation[9] has started human trials (May 2004) to see if a compound found in turmeric is helpful with the disease. Further research reveals that Curcumin might be helpful with multiple sclerosis[10] also.

I read that Curcumin which is a chemical found in turmeric can help fight off malaria infections.[11] *Pete, UK*

Liver

Turmeric aids the liver in doing its cleansing job by helping the detoxifying process and protecting the liver.

Osteoarthritis may be helped by turmeric because it is an anti-inflammatory.[12] *Susan, Denmark*

Caution

Don't use turmeric if you suffer from gallstones or bile duct problems – its use could cause gallbladder problems.

Peppermint

- Latin name: *Mentha piperita*
- Relieves muscle spasms
- Increases sweating
- Stimulates secretion of bile
- Antiseptic

Indigestion

Peppermint calms the muscles of the stomach and improves the flow of bile, which the body uses to digest fats.

As a result, food passes through the stomach more quickly.

If your symptoms of indigestion are related to a condition called gastoesophageal reflux disease or GERD, peppermint should not be used.

Flatulence

Peppermint relaxes the muscles that allow the body to rid itself of painful digestive gas.

Tension headache

Research has shown that peppermint applied to the forehead and temples compares favourably with acetaminophen (a commonly used over-the-counter medication) in terms of its ability to reduce headache symptoms.

A 1995 double blind, placebo-controlled study determined that essential oil (always dilute) of peppermint rubbed into the forehead might be an effective tension-headache treatment capable of relaxing muscles and relieving pain.[13]

Nausea

Peppermint can help to reduce nausea and can also be helpful for travel sickness.

A British study found that peppermint oil is a potentially useful therapy for preventing the nausea that often occurs after a surgical operation.[14]

Fevers

The sweating powers of peppermint are good for helping the body to regulate temperatures particularly for flu and fevers.

Nasal congestion

Rubbing a few drops of diluted peppermint oil on your palms and chest is a good remedy for blocked nasal passages.

Peppermint is an excellent 'winter' herb. I have used it for many years for colds, flu and keeping warm. *Fran, UK*

Caution

Do not give the herb to children under 5. Also essential oil should not be prescribed for children under 12. Do not take the essential oil internally. Always dilute.

Furthermore peppermint oil should not be used by anyone with serious gallbladder inflammation, obstruction of the bile ducts, or severe liver disease. Those with gallstones should consult a physician before using peppermint oil.

Lavender

- Latin name: *Lavandula officinalis*
- Carminative[15]
- Relieves muscle spasms
- Antidepressant
- Antiseptic
- Antibacterial
- Stimulates blood flow

Depression

Lavender is well known for its calming and soothing effects. It can also be used to calm the nerves and relieve irritability. A small clinical study suggested that lavender is helpful for mild depression.[16]

Sleeplessness

Lavender is often combined with other sedative type herbs to aid restful sleep. A few drops in a bath or on a pillow at night will encourage a good night's sleep.

Antiseptic

Lavender is a strong antiseptic and so is quite good for burns, wounds and sores.

A few drops massaged into the temples is said to ease headaches.

Asthma

Being a relaxing herb, lavender helps asthma sufferers, particularly if their suffering has a 'nervous' component.

Digestion

Colic, indigestion, wind and bloating are all helped by a lavender infusion.

Caution

Do not take lavender essential oil internally.

Celery

- Latin name: *Apium graveolens*
- Diuretic
- Anti-rheumatic
- Urinary antiseptic
- Lowers blood pressure

Detoxifying

You can make a fantastically nutritious cleansing juice from celery that helps to detoxify the body. The seeds help the kidneys dispose of unwanted waste products and reduce the acidity in the whole body, which also alleviates arthritis.

> I detox every six months. One of the main ingredients in my juices is celery along with other green vegetables. Use carrots to sweeten the juice.
> *Paul J, USA*

Disinfection

Celery seeds make an effective treatment for cystitis (inflammation of the bladder often caused by bacterial infections) because it is highly antiseptic and mildly diuretic.

Circulation

Celery seeds have been known to improve the circulation of blood to muscles and joints.

Chest infections

Using celery seeds in herbal remedies has been known to be beneficial for conditions such as asthma and bronchitis.

Blood pressure

A research study[20] concluded that people with high blood pressure should eat up to four ribs of celery a day.

> A compound found in celery, 3-n-butyl phthalide, has been shown experimentally to lower blood pressure.

Caution

Do not take medicinally if pregnant or suffering from a kidney disorder. Do not use celery seeds that are sold for cultivation purposes. Do not take essential oil internally.

Thyme

- Latin name: *Thymus vulgaris*
- Bactericidal (antiseptic)
- Can be used to treat colds, coughs and flu
- Helps with asthma
- Emmenagogue[21]
- Soothes muscle aches
- Expectorant

Candles

Interestingly, adding thyme, as well as other (orange, eucalyptus) essential oils, to candles has a powerful bactericidal effect,[22] when the herb is dispersed into the air and combines with ions produced in the flame (of the candle).

Essential oil

Thyme can be used as a chest rub, massage oil, or on wounds or stings.

> Oils are often concentrated and so remember to (well) dilute them in a carrier, e.g. water. *Janice, UK*

Whooping cough, bronchitis and pleurisy are all remedied by a thyme infusion. The infusion can be taken for minor chest and throat infections.

> You can chew the leaves of thyme to relieve sore throats. Fran, USA

Hay fever and asthma

For those who suffer from asthma the use of thyme, as well as other herbs, is recommended. Its invigorating qualities help with the sedating effects of other herbs used for asthma. The symptoms of hay fever are also relieved by thyme infusions.

Back pain

Massaging a little thyme oil into your body helps tired and aching muscles, muscle spasms and back pain.

> A tincture of thyme is an excellent remedy for diarrhoea.[23] *Sarah, Italy*

Putting thyme paste on your skin helps bites and stings. Also helps against ringworms, athlete's foot, scabies and lice.

Caution
Don't take if pregnant, and don't take essential oil internally.

Ginseng

- Latin name: *Panax ginseng*
- Improves stamina
- Immune system
- Cures insomnia
- Can treat nervous exhaustion
- Tonic
- Adaptogenic[24]

Adaption
Ginseng helps the body adapt to stress and fatigue. It is also a tonic against extremes of temperature.

Stress
Both emotional and mental stresses are aided by the use of ginseng herb.

My sister has been suffering from emotional stress for many years. It is only recently that I learned of herbs that could help with her stress. She swears by ginseng tea now. *Angela, USA*

Memory
A cup of ginseng tea is an excellent herbal drink for coping with the stress of exams or moving home.

Ginseng improves memory and may also be helpful with improving the memory of stroke patients.[25] *Debbie J, UK*

Sleep problems
If you're feeling sleepy but can't get to sleep – then try ginseng – it acts like a sedative in cases of fatigue.

American ginseng is more of a sedative than most other types (of ginseng). *Kieran, Ireland*

Sugar levels

Research[26] is suggesting that ginseng or an extract from ginseng berries is helpful in reducing sugar levels in diabetics as well as helping in reducing weight.

Stamina

Ginseng is best known as a stimulant tonic herb for athletes and those subject to physical stress. In this regard ginseng improves stamina.

> Ginseng in soup is an excellent way to add this herb to your health repertoire. Add 1 g of dried root to a bowl of soup as a general tonic. *Jenny, China*

Cautions

Do not exceed dosage given by your herbalist. Do not take for more than 6 weeks. Avoid caffeine when taking ginseng. Do not use if pregnant.

St John's wort

- Latin name: *Hypericum perforatum*
- Antidepressant
- Antispasmodic
- Sedative
- Antiviral
- Astringent

Nervous problems

Herbalists have used St Johns wort for treating nervous problems such as anxiety, tension, insomnia and depression.

> I always try a herbal solution for patients suffering from depression, before I resort to drugs. St John's wort is my first choice.[27] *Dr Beverly D, UK*

Hormones

St John's wort helps menopausal problems. Try ½ tsp with water. This is also a tonic for liver and gallbladder problems.

Bites

This herb is good for treating wounds, insect bites and burns.

Cramps

St John's wort helps to relieve cramps and nerve pain.

Ulcers

St John's wort is known to be helpful in treating ulcers.[28] Also helps with colic, gastric inflammation and peptic ulcers. Take as an infused oil.

Infections

The whole herb is effective against viral infections such as chicken pox, shingles and cold sores. Researchers[29] are looking into its use against major viruses such as HIV.

Caution

May cause sensitivity to sunlight. It is restricted in a few countries.

Holy basil

- Latin name: *Ocimum sanctum*
- Lowers blood sugar
- Antispasmodic
- Reduces fever
- Lowers blood pressure
- Anti-inflammatory

Invigoration

Holy basil is known as an invigorating herb tonic, in this regard it has been used to lift the spirit and improve vitality.

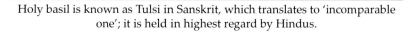

Holy basil is known as Tulsi in Sanskrit, which translates to 'incomparable one'; it is held in highest regard by Hindus.

Stress

The herb has healing properties that could help people with high blood pressure and cholesterol levels. The herb is considered 'adaptogenic' in that it helps the body adapt to new demands.

Diabetes

A research study[30] showed that holy basil helped lower blood sugar levels in type 2 diabetics. This was further encouraged by the suggestion that it could be used to help diabetics who were on dietary therapy.

Coughs and sneezes

Respiratory infections such as colds, coughs, bronchitis and pleurisy are all helped by holy basil.

> I am an Ayurvedic practitioner and have used the herb holy basil to treat asthma sufferers. *Carol, USA*

Ayurvedic medicine

According to Ayurvedic medicine the juice of holy basil can be applied to bites and stings. Also it can be used for ringworm and skin problems.

> The juice or powder of holy basil is helpful for mouth ulcers. *Carol, USA*

White willow

- Latin name: *Salix alba*
- Analgesic
- Anti-inflammatory
- Reduces fever
- Antirheumatic
- Astringent[31]

Headaches

Some conventional headache medications have been known to have several side effects, such as stomach irritation and even causing ulcers.

Studies[32] suggest that white willow is preferable to drug therapies in relieving headaches.

> White willow bark was used as pain relief long before aspirin was discovered.

Hot conditions

Traditional herbal medicines recommend white willow for fevers and other 'hot' conditions.

> Willow is an excellent remedy for reducing fever chills and managing high fevers. *Paul, USA*

> Hot flushes and night sweats can be helped by a willow tincture.
> *Sharon, France*

Mobility

White willow is an excellent remedy for arthritic and rheumatic pain.

> Particularly if it is in the back, knees or hips. *Delia, UK*

In combination with other herbs, it helps relieve swelling and inflammation. Some people have reported an increase in mobility.

Caution

Do not use if allergic to aspirin. Also avoid if pregnant or breast-feeding.

Elder

- Latin name: *Sambucus nigra*
- Increases sweating
- Diuretic[33]
- Anti-inflammatory

Colds

Coughs, colds and flu are all helped by an infusion of elder made from the flowering tops.

> I have a large family and always keep a fresh infusion of elderflower handy for winter blues. *Sarah, Canada*

Elder produces a mild perspiration that helps reduce fevers.

Constipation

Elderberries are a mild laxative and contain antiviral properties. For this reason they are often used for diarrhoea and constipation.

Hay fever

It has been reported that an infusion of elder taken often, and leading up to the hay fever season, can help prevent this condition.

Catarrh

Chronic catarrh and ear infections have also been treated by the use of a tincture made from the tops of the elderflower.

Caution

Although some recommend using the bark, this may cause side effects, so only use the flowers and berries.

Ginger

- Latin name: *Zingiber officinalis*
- Anti-emetic
- Stimulates circulation
- Antiseptic
- Anti-inflammatory
- Inhibits coughing

Trapped wind

Indigestion, wind and colic are all remedied by the use of a ginger tincture. Take 30 drops with water twice a day.

Taken internally, ginger is also good for gastro-intestinal infections since it has some antiseptic qualities.

Cancer

Recently, researchers have become increasingly interested in ginger as an aid to blocking cancer. In particular, they have been concentrating on its effects on bowel cancer...

> Scientists suspect that gingerol, which gives ginger its flavour, may help in protecting against bowel cancer ... recent studies are showing notable cancer prevention potential with the use of ginger.

> The ginger family has been used for thousands of years in the treatment and prevention of various illnesses, and has been hypothesized to have anti-cancer[34] and therapeutic properties.

> Plants of the ginger family have been credited with therapeutic and preventive powers and have been reported to have anti-bowel cancer[35] activity.

Travel sickness

Ginger is an excellent remedy against travel sickness and nausea. Take a few ginger sweets or ginger biscuits when travelling and you will not have any problems.

> Ginger has proven better than other drugs for post-operative nausea.

Colds and flu

Ginger increases sweating and reduces fever and it is warming and soothing for coughs, colds, flu and respiratory ailments.

> I am a practitioner of Chinese medicine and I recommend ginger for chills and aching muscles. *May, UK*

> Warm water, some ground ginger, a teaspoon of honey and a squeeze of lemon, makes a nice drink and is good for so many things. *Irene, UK*

Research

Can ginger increase the metabolic rate and improve circulation in the hands and feet? A study is underway (2004) at Reading University[36] to find out.

Heart

Thromboxanes are a major cause of clogged arteries. While many doctors recommend a daily intake of aspirin to remedy this build-up, a group of researchers at Cornell Medical School[37] found ginger to be as effective as aspirin.

Also it was found that ginger's antioxidant constituents strengthened the cardiac muscle, while studies in Japan and India have shown that ginger lowers serum cholesterol levels by interfering with cholesterol biosynthesis.

Caution

Do not take in medicinal doses if suffering from peptic ulcers. Do not take the essential oil internally.

Echinacea

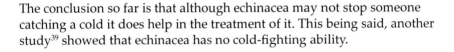

- Latin name: *Echinacea angustifolia*
- Heals wounds
- Anti-inflammatory
- Antibiotic
- Anti-allergenic
- Detoxifying

Colds and flu

Several studies[38] have been conducted to determine the cold and flu-fighting abilities of echinacea.

The conclusion so far is that although echinacea may not stop someone catching a cold it does help in the treatment of it. This being said, another study[39] showed that echinacea has no cold-fighting ability.

Stimulation

Echinacea stimulates the immune system and is particularly helpful in fighting chronic infections. It makes a good treatment for myalgic encephalopathy (post-viral fatigue syndrome).

Respiratory illnesses

Hay fever, asthma, and other respiratory illnesses can be treated with echinacea.

AIDS and HIV

Several sources[40] report that people suffering from HIV use echinacea because of its stimulating effects on the immune system.

However this advice is to be taken with caution as echinacea may have debilitating effects on the body's cells.

Infections

When taken with other herbs, such as buchu, echinacea is helpful in treating urinary tract and kidney infections.

I have used echinacea to help clear up skin infections. *Carla, USA*

In this regard it is also used for wounds and skin regeneration.[41]

Research

The most consistently proven[42] effect of echinacea is in stimulating 'phagocytosis', that is encouraging white blood cells and lymphocytes to attack invading organisms.

Caution

Do not use echinacea for long periods of time. Two weeks on and one week off should be a good guide. Also, high doses may cause dizziness and nausea.

Sage

- Latin name: *Salvia officinalis*
- Astringent
- Antiseptic
- Oestrogenic
- Reduces sweating
- Tonic

Mouth

The astringent and anti-septic properties of sage make this warm, slightly bitter-tasting herb ideal for almost all types of sore throats, mouth infections and sore gums.

Bites and stings

Rubbing the leaves or juice directly onto bites, stings and minor swellings can be helpful.

Traditionally speaking, sage has been used in smoking mixtures to help asthmatics.

Calm

In Chinese medicine sage is used as a tonic that both calms and stimulates the nervous system.

Menstruation

Sage encourages the flow of menstrual blood, making it useful for those who have irregular periods. It also helps reduce period pain. During the menopause, sage is helpful in regulating the hormones.

Memory

Research[43] suggests that sage is good for memory recall. In a study it was shown that subjects given sage oil tablets performed better at memory recall tests than those given a placebo. Building on this evidence, new research is being conducted to see if sage can have a positive effect on Alzheimer's sufferers.[44]

Caution

Do not take if pregnant or epileptic.

Liquorice

- Latin name: *Glycyrrhiza glabra*
- Anti-inflammatory
- Expectorant
- Demulcent
- Mild laxative

Digestive system

Inflammatory conditions of the digestive system are soothed by liquorice. Thus this herb relieves such conditions as mouth ulcers, gastritis, peptic ulceration and acid problems.

Liver

A key ingredient of liquorice, glycyrrhizin, is quite effective at treating cirrhosis of the liver and chronic hepatitis.

Liquorice root has been used in Japan for years to treat liver diseases.
Sarah, Japan[45]

Liquorice also reduces the breakdown of steroids by the liver and kidneys (steroids are natural or synthetic substances that regulate body function).

Constipation

Liquorice is a gentle laxative that can help ease constipation, particularly if combined with other herbs, such as dandelion and yellow dock.

Expectorant

In ancient Greece, liquorice was taken to ease conditions of asthma, coughs and bronchitis.

> I have used powdered dried root for coughs and it worked fine. Sweet as well! *Joanne, UK*

Adrenal glands

Some research[46] suggests that liquorice helps people with adrenal gland failure (Addison's[47] disease). The research suggests that liquorice stimulates the adrenal gland.

> This research is not conclusive and most doctors still recommend that you stay away from liquorice if you suffer from Addison's.

Arthritis

As an anti-inflammatory, liquorice is good for inflamed joints and arthritis sufferers.

Caution

Don't take if pregnant, anaemic or blood pressure is elevated.

Aloe vera

- Latin name: *Aloe vera*
- Heals wounds
- Emollient[48]
- Stimulates secretion of bile
- Laxative
- Calms varicose veins

Cleopatra

It is suggested that Cleopatra attributed her beauty to the virtues of aloe vera. This herb is famed for its inclusion in beauty products.

Several studies[49] have suggested that aloe vera has a soothing and nurturing effect on the skin.

Irritable bowel syndrome

There has been some research that suggests that aloe vera is helpful in relieving irritable bowel syndrome.[50] A gel formed from aloe vera is also helpful for peptic ulcers.

Laxative

Bitter aloes (the bitter yellow liquid in the leaves) is a strong laxative that causes the colon to contract, usually causing a bowel movement within 8 to 12 hours.

Burns, grazes and scalds

For burns, scalds, grazes and sunburn; a leaf, broken off, releases a soothing gel that may be applied to the affected part.

My home med-kit has a solution of aloe vera that comes in very handy when you have kids dashing around the home and garden, and for me when I am on one of my DIY frenzies. *John, D*

Diabetes

A few studies have shown that aloe vera juice was helpful in reducing blood sugar levels of diabetics. Furthermore the studies also showed a drop in triglycerides.[51]

All-rounder

Several small studies[52] hint at the benefits of aloe vera for helping with killing parasites and to treat angina, diabetes, hepatitis and psoriasis.

Cautions

Do not use bitter aloes on the skin. Do not take if pregnant or suffering from haemorrhoids or kidney disease.

Figwort

- Latin name: *Scrophularia nodosa*
- Mild laxative
- Lymphatic cleanser
- Diuretic

Anti-inflammatory

Figwort is useful for inflammatory skin conditions such as eczema and psoriasis. It is particularly effective where the condition is chronic and there has been a discharge.

Burns and swelling

The bruised leaves have been used as a poultice for burns and swelling.

Pain

Figwort is mildly anodyne (i.e. has pain relieving properties) when applied to the skin.

Caution

Should be avoided by people who suffer from tachycardia (a rapid heartbeat) and other heart conditions.

Rosemary

- Latin name: *Rosmarinus officianlis*
- Antispasmodic
- Anti-fungal
- Antibacterial

Stimulation

Rosemary is a stimulant that helps the flow of blood, increasing the flow so that the blood can easily reach the extremities of the body as well as the brain. It also helps to strengthen capillary walls.

Rheumatism

Rosemary has some pain-relieving properties when applied to the skin and is good for mild rheumatic pain in joints and muscles.

Digestion

Rosemary helps the digestive system and increases the flow of bile (the digestive juice that is released by the liver); this juice helps with digestion and ridding the body of waste.

Nervous tension

Rosemary is a fairly decent remedy for depression and anxiety, particularly if this is associated with nervous tension.

Combining rosemary with lavender is an excellent bathing solution.
Janice, UK

Hair tonic

Scalp conditions such as hair loss and dandruff can be alleviated by washing with rosemary soap.

Caution

Avoid during pregnancy since rosemary is a strong uterine stimulant.

Herbs for children

In this section I want to look at some of the typical childhood illnesses that can be helped by herbs.

Anxiety and stress

A camomile infusion is good for children who are over excited, stressful or anxious. This infusion will help them to calm down and also aid a restful sleep.

Also useful is a warm bath with a mix of lavender and camomile. Don't add the herbs to the bath; instead add some (herbs) to a pan then add water, boil and allow to steep for 20 minutes. Now strain the water into the bath.

Chickenpox and measles

The itching caused by this illness is almost unbearable. Use a decoction of chickweed, comfrey and rosemary to help relieve itching.

Colds

Using a steam inhalation of tea tree, peppermint, lavender or eucalyptus will help some of the congestion and respiratory problems.

Lice

Lice[18] are a problem that is easily dealt with using a fine-toothed comb and some tea tree oil. Place a few drops on the comb and use it to comb the infected person's hair thoroughly for two weeks.

A mild shampoo of thyme and tea tree oil used every night for a fortnight will deal with the lice problem. *Angie, UK*

Diarrhoea

If this symptom persists (for more than two or three days) then seek medical attention. A mild infusion of rosemary, meadowsweet and raspberry leaves will help relieve this condition.

A compound[53] found in blueberries helps to clear up diarrhoea.

Colic

First, and foremost, if your baby is crying a lot then call the doctor! Get the baby checked out to ensure that nothing serious is going on.

As far as herbal remedies go, a combination of camomile, fennel, vervain, liquorice and balm-mint was found to be effective in one study.[54]

Teething

This can be soothed using an infusion of camomile or lemon balm. Make the infusion mild.

Cooking

Herbs have been used for millennia as flavourings and additions to cooking. In the table below I have come up with a selection of culinary herbs and their healing properties.

Herb	Cooking	Healing
Marjoram (oregano)	Add fresh to salad dressings and grilled meats.	Circulatory stimulant, digestive aid.
Sage	Cook with strong flavoured meats or use as stuffing.	Helps menopausal problems and is good for digestion and diarrhoea.
Rosemary	To flavour meat dishes or in fresh salads.	Helps depression. Enhances memory and concentration.
Coriander	Soups, stews and curries.	Helps to expel trapped wind, is also disinfecting.
Bay	Soups, casseroles and with rice.	Helps expel trapped wind.
Celery seeds	Enhance flavour of soups, stews and omelettes.	Stimulates digestive system. Has a cleansing action.
Parsley	Add to fish, pasta and rice dishes.	Is disinfecting, diuretic and cleansing
Thyme	Use to flavour meats, soups and poultry.	Helps digestive problems and is an expectorant.
Garlic	Sauces, meat dishes, pates and dips.	Helps cardiovascular problems, stimulates digestion.

Care and caution

In this section I want to outline some general cares and cautions that you should be aware of when thinking of herbal remedies.

- Be aware that more is not necessarily better. Stronger symptoms do not always mean that the herbal remedy should be stronger also.

- Herbs have to go into your system and 'get' to the place they need to be to heal, and so they are likely to take more time than conventional medicine might. Try to support herbal health with patience, diet and exercise.

- Dosage is an important factor with herbs. One dose does not fit all; children for example will have a smaller dose than adults. Not only that but age, weight and medical history must be taken into account too.

- Current medication and diet must be considered when taking herbal remedies. Many people eat herbs as part of their diet; a good example being ginger. These and the medication that you maybe taking must be considered carefully when thinking of herbal health.

Finally, herbs can be dangerous, addictive, and toxic. Treat them with care and the respect they deserve and they will stand you in good stead.

Final words

Please remember that herbs should be respected at all times. Always seek the advice of a professional and accredited herbalist and always consult your physician. Knowledge is power! So ask questions.

It is difficult to change herb lore as it is ingrained in centuries of tradition. Scientific research is always bringing up new and interesting findings. Hence it is important to keep an eye out for new research at all times.

I always delight in hearing readers' healing tales, so please visit the website below and let me know how you use herbs to bring well being to the world:

www.healingbooks.net

Go out into the world - look, see, touch, smell and sense the world of herbs. There is a magic that can only be known by experience.

You have taken the first step with this book. I hope that you continue your exploration of herbs.

Thanks for your time

Kal

The websites mentioned below were correct at the time of going to press. Due to the volatile nature of the Internet I cannot guarantee that the information on these websites is correct or still exists.

Always be careful when trusting information found on the internet.

Endnotes:

[1] A substance that stimulates removal of mucous from the lungs

[2] University of Maryland Medical Center: *www.umm.edu/altmed/ConsConditions/IntestinalParasitescc.html*

[3] Wright State University: *www.wright.edu/admin/fredwhite/pharmacy/popular_nremedies.html*

[4] The Garlic Information Centre: *www.garlic.mistral.co.uk/cholest.htm*

[5] BBC News 07/11/2002: *news.bbc.co.uk/1/hi/health/2415035.stm*

[6] News Target: *www.newstarget.com/008124.html*

[7] Gilroy Garlic Festival: *www.gilroygarlicfestival.com/*

[8] BBC News: *news.bbc.co.uk/1/hi/health/1668932.stm*

[9] *www.mercola.com/2004/may/5/turmeric_spice.htm*

[10] *www.mult-sclerosis.org/news/Apr2002/CurrySpiceForMS.html*

[11] New Scientist: *www.newscientist.com/channel/health/mg18524812.100*

[12] University of Maryland Medical Center: *www.umm.edu/altmed/ConsHerbs/Turmericch.html*

[13] Göbel H, G. Schmidt, M. Dworshak, et al. Essential plant oils and headache mechanisms. Phytomedicine. 1995; 2(2):93-102

[14] Tate, S., "Peppermint oil: a treatment for postoperative nausea," J Adv Nurs (1997), 26(3):543-49

[15] Carminative means: a substance that stops the formation of intestinal gas and helps expel gas that has already formed

[16] US Nat.Lib.Med: *www.nlm.nih.gov/medlineplus/druginfo/natural/patient-lavender.html*

[17] Hardy M, Kirk-Smith MD, Stretch DD. Replacement of drug therapy for insomnia by ambient odour. Lancet 1995;346:701 [letter].

[18] *www.homemakingcottage.com/health/lice.html*

[19] Blumenthal M, Busse WR, Goldberg A, et al. (eds). The Complete Commission E Monographs: Therapeutic Guide to Herbal Medicines. Boston, MA: Integrative Medicine Communications, 1998, 159–60.

[20] *www.whfoods.com/genpage.php?tname=disease&dbid=15*

[21] Emmenagogue means increases menstrual discharge

[22] University of Southampton: *www.soton.ac.uk/mediacentre/news/2004/june/04_89.shtml*

[23] eNotes: *health.enotes.com/alternative-medicine-encyclopedia/thyme*

[24] Adaptogenic herbs help you adapt to changes in life, environment and may increase stamina and sports performance.

[25] Amer Stroke Assc: *www.strokeassociation.org/presenter.jhtml?identifier=3008845*

[26] American Diabetes Association - see our site link

[27] BBC News: *news.bbc.co.uk/1/hi/health/4255087.stm*

[28] Herb Research Foundation: *www.herbs.org/herbpacketsummariesR-Z.htm*

[29] Medicine Net: *www.medicinenet.com/script/main/art.asp?articlekey=55083*

[30] Journ. clinincal pharmacology and therapeutics *www.ncbi.nlm.nih.gov/entrez/query.fcgi?cmd=Retrieve&db=PubMed&list_uids=8880292&dopt=Abstract*

[31] Astringent: A substance that shrinks body tissues

[32] University of Maryland: *www.umm.edu/altmed/ConsHerbs/WillowBarkch.html*

[33] Diuretic: A substance that increases the flow of urine from the body

[34] American Assoc. of Cancer Research: *www.aacr.org/Default.aspx?p=2084&d=193*

[35] BBC News: *news.bbc.co.uk/1/hi/health/3221547.stm*

[36] Reading University: *www.extra.rdg.ac.uk/news/details.asp?ID=388*

[37] N.E. Journal of Medicine, 1980: *content.nejm.org/*

[38] Univ. Maryland: *www.umm.edu/altmed/ConsHerbs/Echinaceach.html*

[39] BBC News: *news.bbc.co.uk/1/hi/health/3256026.stm*

[40] AIDS Info Net: *www.aidsinfonet.org/articles.php?articleID=726*

[41] Herb Research Foundation: *www.herbs.org/greenpapers/echinacea.html*

[42] Echinacea Articles: *www.chiro.org/nutrition/echinacea.shtml*

[43] BBC News: *news.bbc.co.uk/1/hi/health/3189635.stm*

[44] HealthierLife: *www.thehealthierlife.co.uk/article/2940/alzheimers-disease.html*

[45] HealthWorld: *www.healthy.net/scr/article.asp?lk=P598&Id=1319*

[46] MedLinePlus: *www.nlm.nih.gov/medlineplus/druginfo/natural/patient-licorice.html*

[47] Addison's Group: *www.adshg.org.uk/*

[48] Emollient means: An agent that softens and soothes the skin when applied locally

[49] *www.internethealthlibrary.com/Plant-Remedies/AloeVera.htm*

[50] *gut.bmjjournals.com/cgi/content/full/50/suppl_2/a82*

[51] Yongchaiyudha S, Rungpitarangsi V, Bunyapraphatsara N, et al. Antidiabetic activity of Aloe vera juice. I Clinical trial in new cases of diabetes mellitus. Phytomedicine 1996; 3,3:241-243

[52] *www.internethealthlibrary.com/Plant-Remedies/AloeVera-research.htm#Aloe%20Vera%20and%20wound%20care*

[53] *www.blueberry.org/health.htm*

[54] Weizman Z, Alkrinawi S, Goldfarb D, et al. Efficacy of herbal tea preparation in infantile colic. Journal of Pediatrics 122(1993):650-2.